My Rapport with the Spirit of Dr. Albert Einstein

~ TIMEISM ~

NEUTRAL UNIVERSE

THE TIMING REVOLUTION

The Journey

My Rapport with the Spirit of Dr. Albert Einstein

Edmond Cohen

Edited by
Pablo Capra
Chris Jones

G.U.T.
Quantum Mechanics

T.O.E.
General Relativity

A SERIES SPONSORED BY
www.universityoftime.com

Firing Thoughts

TIMEISM

20/21 Vision ~ Edmond Cohen

www.universityoftime.com

zeroonetime@gmail.com

Book Design: Edmond Cohen and Pablo Capra

PRINTED IN THE USA

~ ~ ~

TIMING

Contents

My Rapport with the Spirit of Einstein

a book of blooming ideas
of the Collective Human Mind

God is neutral, suspended
between past and future

Natural Intelligence

Thoughts devour
thoughts

0
1
0

On/0ff
Neutral
Switching
From 0 flickering to a
010 dimensional mind
Baby Bangs create Bigger Bangs
Cooperation is the Measure of Success

Now you don't need to read the book

∞^2=Timing=mc^2

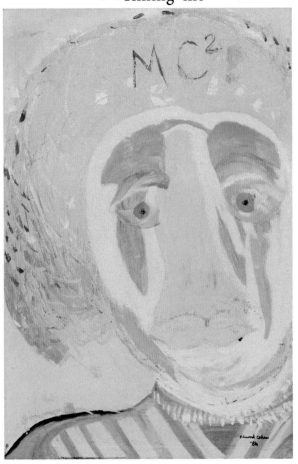

Mind Capacity Squared

Painting by the Author

mc²

The Spirit of Relativity

$$\infty^2 = \text{Timing} = mc^2$$

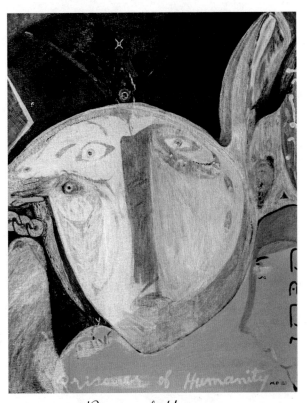

Prisoner of Humanity

Painting by the Author

∞^2

The Author Suspended in Time

We are a Quantum Timing Machine

Genesis ~ the Life Force
Understand God ~ not the God Particle

In the beginning there was a conspiratorial ancient quantum mechanics Code, called Yahweh.

יה~וה
Time
Past & future
Creation ~ Evolution ~ Entropy

Creation evolves, forming and reforming Informing us to grasp the coded Mind of God's potential, to be discovered by the mysterious grace of the dualistic 01 Quantum Singularity, leading the Quantum exchange between the polarities of Electro ~ Magnetism.

Reading this book will assist you to focus on your life's goals for joy, comfort, and fulfilment.

The theory herein will refresh and enhance your telepathic receptors, your resilient mind-power informing you to attend to the Neutral / Nature of the dualistic Intangible-Tangible Timing universe. The Time ~ Timing ~ universe in need to be understood the cosmic split formation of telepathic synapses, enhancing our humanistic communication, enabling us to understand the Neutral forces of our existence. Like Ai, and GPS, the singular force of 'God's' Creation.

Einstein's quotes below have been quantized to affect your mind, to help you understand God's Creation, rather than Believing in Voodooism.

Here I'll present to you one of the most mind-rattling quotes from one of the most celebrated Men/Gods in the annals of history, Dr. Albert Einstein.

Dr. Einstein has had many great scientific and philosophical Ideas that helped humanity to understand 99% physics and 1% philosophical dilemma.

Moreover, Dr. Einstein would have been pleased to learn about the utilization of Quantum physics to reach a new crescendo, to search for the next mental filling station, to augment the missing telepathic juices in the collective human Mind.

~~~

Throughout the following conversation with the spirited Master-Mind Dr. Albert Einstein. Here I will share with you the basic General relativity ~ coupled with some bits and bytes of the Information

System, which can help you connect the dots between the ongoing millennia of the **justified** and the **un**justified wars of attrition between religions.

The world has been afflicted with mentally depraved children who grew up to instigate wars and violence, ending in a grave-digging to bury those who fought for Truth, peace and quality of life.

Guess who won and lost all of humanity's historic wars?

Wars have been raging forever between the Positive and the Negative forces of nature ~ and in between the Light and the Dark forces of the human mind.

This book will guide you through the Universal G.U.T. and T.O.E. of Matter and Energy; the initial Creation and the Evolutionary understanding of Electro Magnetism, and thermodynamics.

Here you will read about the humanistic advisor and eminent philosopher of the 20th century, Dr. Albert Einstein.

A cautionary note before proceeding to read the Tzimtzum below:

When I first read this Tzimtzum translation published by AGADAH magazine some 42 years ago I had to read it several times before I could grasp the seminal Enormity of its meaning. It helped me synchronize my imagination of an uncharted map to guide my primordial feelings by unlocking the volt of my vast memories, and my Genetic Makeup.

Today, Quantum Physics reveals the immense philosophical implications for future generations, and become masters of their own Beingness. Their thoughts will be of self-acknowledgment, and recite the adage: "I am that I am" as we all are born the same, but different.

The Tzimtzum translation below was rendered by the Chasidic Rabbi David Din, quantifying the complex Kabbalistic meaning as to how the expanding and contracting Universe works.
From A to Z, from 0 to 1. Information Theory of the Information System. IT will give you a vivid comprehension of the Kabbalistic Celestial Truth.

From *Likutei Halachot* by Rebbi Nussan of Nemi-
rov, rendered
by Dovid Din

In the writings of the holy Ari, the master of the
Kabbalah, there is explained the deep mystery of
the "contractions" which occurred before the Creation, before even the beginning of the world of the
supernal emanations—how he, be he blessed!
Contracted the pure light of his spiritual essence in
order that the great void should be created, an
empty space into which the Creation might issue
forth. And even so, within this world of the contractions were many and diverse levels of descending
being. And ever so gradually as the thin shaft of
the divine light began its long, long descent into
the gaping void, different facets and brilliances of
the light became apparent as the forms of Creation began to rise slowly out of the formlessness.
And in its turn, each measured facet of that light
contracted and expanded many Times over until
the world of emanations, *Atzilus* the cabbalists call
it, came about, so the process of contractions and
expansions repeated itself, over and over again
compressing and expanding, inhaling and exhal-
ing, embracing the pain of withdrawal and the joy

of flowing outward again until emerged all the levels of being, *B'riah*-Creation, *Yetzirah*-formation, and finally the dark, shadowy world of our reality, *Assiyah*-activity. And here, on this very lowest rung, is set man, who with his simple power of choosing and perceiving the supreme good is capable of shattering the illusion of activity, reversing the flow back to where everything is sustained in the divine unity. And this is the essential task of the Jew, returning all things to their resolution in the beatific vision of the one, thereby all the extensions, all the anguish and pain and suffering, which is really the divine light contracting and compressing itself in the narrowness of our Time and our place, will be repaired: and all this depends on our inner seeing and believing and the choices we make, restoring all things to their place and releasing the divine light hidden within.

Expansion ~ Contraction ~~ Light and Dark

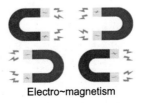

Electro~magnetism

On that note,

please Join us as we stand on the shoulders of historic giants:

The Quanta
Light as Dark
Abraham of Ur
Galileo Galilei
Isaac Newton
Einstein

Creation
Thought
God
iQ
~
=

Electro ~ magnetism
Quantum simulation
singular ~ universe

Quantum ~ Reality
10 dimensional
Time
!
-

יה~וה
Yahweh

Now, let us shine the spotlight on the Spirit of the human God Dr. Albert Einstein whose mind is still roaming among the brightest living stars.

Note:
Einstein's quotes are in *Italic Black,*
and my rapport in random colors.

Time Creates
Entropy Destroys

Here is another first and the second *salvo*
still reverberating from
the cannon-mind of Dr. Albert Einstein;
Mind Capacity Squared

=

MC2

First salvo:
We are slowed down sound and light waves, a walking bundles of frequencies tuned into the cosmos. We are souls dressed in sacred biochemical garments and our bodies are the instruments through which our souls play their music.

Second salvo:
A man who is convinced of the truth of his religion is indeed never tolerant. At the least, he is to feel pity for the adherent of another religion but usually it does not stop there. The faithful adherent of a religion will try first of all to convince those that believe in another religion and usually he goes on to hatred if he is not successful. However, hatred then leads to persecution when the might of the majority is behind it.

Absolutely clear, Doctor,
We are all as Bio-degradable as all Matter and Energy, can Be, Light and Dark roaming the entropic cosmic to extinction.

"Black holes are where God divided by zero."

—

I view the zero as the Genesis of Thoughts running through the prisms of telepathic kaleido-scopes

The zero I.S. the Universal Master code to the T.E.N. Dimensional Universe

The Eternal Now phenomenon

Zer0 contains the entire Universe
Everything is being created from 0 to Entropy. the Quantum Potential of Creation and Evolution. From Time to Timing all at once.

Now we can have a clear map of the ever expand-ing Quantum Universe so to understand our per-petual illusions.

A new mathematics can split a singularity and peer into its ephemeral ~ x changing reality, only to find that all things emanate out of nothing.
010

o Nothing can spare your prayer

"The most beautiful experience we can have is the mysterious."

——

True, totality cannot be any less mysterious and more beautiful than the collective human mind.
The I.S. ~ is no less mysterious than a God who's hiding in the biggest and the Blackest Hole of darkness, and can still see the light at the end of the tunnel.

Every move I make is a moment of Creation.

Contemplate on your telepathic consciousness that can imagine a 01 Totality.

Thoughts should not be viewed as an absurd beyond the mysterious. Thoughts are as mysterious and glamorous as innate mental algorithms; called Time~ism.
Timing the Total Mind redeems me from accepting any future *response-abilities* for my random thoughts and actions.

I'm only response ~ able.

"The most incomprehensible thing about the world is that it is at all comprehensible."

———

When I subdue my mind to a zero, I can then comprehend the Universe from the outside in.

The mind of God comprehends the self total Being both ways, from the inside out and from the outside in.

A spooky act at cosmic distance.

Imagine 0 nothing as the deepest
hole in the **01 whole** of eternity
where the God Particle IS hiding

"Any fool can know. The point is to understand."
———

Knowledge is the precursor to hermetic understanding as to how Genesis manifest and evolve. Light and dark is our navigational map to a cosmos teaming with little-known photonic quanta and their mechanical Baby Bangs ~ banging Quantum Mechanics ~.

The Universe composed of Q bits, constantly forming bigger Q bytes as tangible matter and energy. Bits and Bytes are a cosmic switch, switching the 0n/0f formations of merging singularities.

Beliefs Systems are born of scattered - segmented truths. We think in terms of yes and no, inhale and exhale as our true reflection on the nature of Timing, and the neutral state of Time~ism.

Quantized Time is the next x change between
Timing and Reality.

No escape and no where to hide
"You are who you are"

Roaming the earth between life and death

"There are only two ways to live your life. One is as though nothing is a miracle. The other is as though everything is a miracle."

———

Creation I.S. the absolute Quantum Miracle.

Everything IS out of nothing, revealed to Father Abraham of Ur on his way to Canaan.
The Genesis concept IS less contentious than the scientific ~ philosophical Quantum Mechanics, and General Relativity. The Consequent discovery of the zero was the second most miraculous event in the annals of human history.

Had there been no Genesis, there would have been no 0s, no Quantum Physics and no General Relativity, and, no Torah to hang our hats on.

Miracles are Magic, living-existence IS one magical miracle; *CREATION IN ACTION*. Every miracle in itself is magical.
Creation IS a white Hole born from the biggest Black Hole of Eternity.

$$1 \; IN \; a \; 0$$

"When the solution is simple, God is answering."

———

I've found Timing to be the simplest mechanism that can match up to God's Ephemeral Beings.

Past and future are but an illusion that can satisfies our orgasmic prayers by whispering God's names, a memorial to life's godly memories.

0 past ~ 1 future.

Go figure who you are and how you can become the acting movie star you aspired to be...

Acting your dualistic personality

"The real goal of my research has always been the simplification and unification of the system of theoretical physics."

———

Sir,
In pursuing the G.U.T. Equation of life's energy, you have touched the flight button of your wildest imagination.

Our massive human difficulty is the acceptance of concepts of the highest magnitude, i.e. the ancient Jewish revelation of Creation; the something out of nothing.
The 010 dualistic system stems from the fact that it is impossible to measure the at-once x measurement of the x change ~ between Matter and Energy.

The Illusionary T.E.N. dimensional measurements exacerbate our inability to extract the bridging Quanta from 0 ~ nothing to 010 Totality

A 010 singularity can observe itself from the inside out, and from the outside in.

As an Ouroboros can

"A person starts to live when he can live outside himself."

—

Spiritually and physically speaking, we are constantly switching in and out, on and 0f, living and dying at the rate of my charming exchanging-genes.

My thoughts are here and in the clouds, they were and still passing by.

In my instantaneous meditative state compels me to repeat a redeeming mantra 'I am not here' It allows me to simply Be ~ regardless of my transient dodo doing at the Time.

Time creates ~ Timing evolves to what
Quantized world of ions really I.S.

Constant Living ~ constant Fading

"Equations are more important to me, because politics is for the present, but an equation is something for eternity.

———

When infinity devours infinity we get a non-polarized neutral equation: Infinity squared ∞^2.

The universe feeds upon itself as Ouroboros do, it feeds upon itself in support of the Universal food chain.

Everything is happening before we can intercept their dualistic meanings:

Time creates – Timing evolves

A neutral 0,10 dimensional universe, between Time and Timing.

How do we measure that?

Time = MC2 = Infinity Squared = I.S.

The 10-Dimensional Universe

"Pure mathematics is, in its way, the poetry of logical ideas."

———

Pure mathematics is the mental resonance of human poetic logic emanating from our standby ~ neural mind, ready to decipher the meanings of Life:

And

the enigma of Mathematical Death

"If A equal success, then the formula is A equal X plus Y and Z, with X being work, Y play, and Z keeping your mouth shut."

———

From A to Z, *I shut my mouth* knowing that science and philosophy are the T.O.E. and the G.U.T. Of the ongoing x changing between dualities.

Our play IS **free** choice. Creativity is the difference between the desirable and the undesirable.

We always act upon our biological-robotic
feelings

We are dodo ~ slaves

(do~do slaves)

We are all biological robots

"I cannot imagine a God who rewards and punishes the objects of his Creation and is but a reflection of human frailty."

———

God is not in the business of reward and punishment. God I.S. a "Being" who has not enough Time to alter the at once Timing of his Creation, the immediate constant of evolutionary x change.

You may believe in God, but it's **healthier** for a well being to **understand** the eminent power of self-Creation. Everything happens bi itself.

Creation IS God. Your thoughts are your God. Your mind is your God.
I do not believe in gods, I put my trust in Godliness. As a biological robot, I am programmed to evolve with God, or without.
Accordingly, don't believe in kings. You my trust in their kingdom.
Don't judge a person, or a nation by their religious beliefs.

Evaluate their creativity, merits, and deeds

Elohim is U

"What really interests me is whether God had any choice in the Creation of the world."

———

Dear Albert,

Your choice and God's choice IS one. A Quantum formation in a 0,10 dimensional Creation and Entropy.

Remember alive or dead, you are the image of God's manifestation.

God said "I am that I am" with no indication as to what the am is. A Neutral entity, no details, zero dimensions, and 0 liabilities.
Fortunately, I discovered the dual God in digital-elves and viruses in my algorithmic coordinates.

Computation is an ephemeral robotic entanglement within the realms of the infinite possibilities, where baby bangs (photons) roam the cosmos, banging our brain's neural grey matter.

Firing mental neutrinos

"There is a race between mankind and the Universe. Mankind is trying to build bigger, better, faster, and more foolproof machines. The Universe is trying to build bigger, better, and faster fools. So far the Universe is winning."

———

God does not race. The universe does the racing. God has no inclination to race against 'discriminatory' races, anyway.
To Be or not to Be, winning or losing, the Universe does not hoot or toot about who wins or who loses.

For millennia, the human race has been racing Vanity Fairs ~ thinking that Evolution can win over Creation. An Impossible feat as both work hand in hand.
If you race to reach up to the image of God, the race has been already won the gambit of our wild Races against the digitized algorithmic Thinking.

Examine your racing thoughts, only to find that there is n0 opponent at the starting gate, except for your own mind, your observer.

Timing I.S. the factor in
Winning and L 00 sing…

"I believe in Spinoza's God, who reveals himself in the "lawful" harmony of the world, not in a God who concerns himself with the fate and the doings of mankind."

———

Yes, Spinoza's God exists in a harmony absent of laws.

God has no concern for the fate of the Universe, or the fate of our religious BS, or even fate of a wild gorilla. Creation I.S. God's only interest.

God conducts all switching energies in an instant. Switching 0n and 0f ~ light and dark ~ zeros and ones all at once.
Things do happen by themselves. God is as in control of human mind as that of an insect's.

God I.S. The total mind, the self-factoring reality, an Ouroboros feeding upon the self. Creation in Action.
Our doings are self-generated abstract within the evolving T.E.N. dimensional God ~ Universe.
To Be or Do…
Is a challenging question to my
inquisitive mind.

"All religions, arts and sciences are branches of the same tree."

——

Do trees talk?

Purportedly the Tree God said to Eve, don't eat from the Tree of Knowledge but failed to mention the Tree of Wisdom, where patience was required, leading to the seasonal - ripened fruit.
But, where do we find the tree of wisdom?

Seasonal wisdom hangs in the balance on the branches of the very tree that bears the fruit of Morality and Ethic, at spooky distance from the Amazonian burning bush, to the melting Polar North, and the drifting Polar South!

Mothers must teach their children morality and ethics; make them to resemble flower buds growing up in a world of joy and passion.

"I am a deeply religious nonbeliever. This is a somewhat new kind of religion."

———

As a nonbeliever, I too, understand totality as my religious escape beyond the ongoing chronic B.S.

As voodoos and Dodos do, so we also have learned to trust in some wheels of fortune as well as trusting in mental delusions.

Luckily I found my refuge by exposing the wild attitude of life experience, musing with Timeism, as the Ideal of my **spiritual ascent** beyond the shedding of my emerging thoughts and feelings.

Where do my thoughts come from?? I have no Idea. I am always ready to face the **neutrino firing squad**, firing God's image into my spirited soul.

Back then, Belief systems and religions were ideal for Hunters and gatherers, as we were not mature enough to grasp the Timing phenomenon.

Primordial Jews had to invent the ephemeral Time so to have an upper hand on political demagogy.

"True religion is real living; living with all one's soul, with all one's goodness and righteousness.

——

A true religion is no religion, and no B.S.

Understanding spiritual life means realizing the non-physical entanglement of the three musketeers; **soul, spirit and mind**, a combination for all aspects of virtual, as well as real beings.

With so mash BS, our living religiously is no longer a K0sher 0ption, other than being *response ~ able*.

Beliefs in sins ~ fasting and regrets, will no longer dominate our obsolete religious denominations.

We must stand under God's religiosity to dispel all politically driven Belief Systems.

(If I fast on Yom Kippur, Ramadan, or on any other day, it is for the sake of tightening my belt to reduce my biomass for optimal efficacy.)

Less is more

"People like us, who believe in physics, know that the distinction between past, present, and future is only a stubbornly persistent illusion."

————

The supernal fate of evolution is the defusing factor of our unbridled wild imagination.

Reality becomes illusion by the natural selection between the rapid x-change in our perception of life and death.

At the end of Time there is no beginning.

Only by dissecting totality will there be a beginning and an end.

Recently, I discovered as how Time has been overrun by Timing, absorbing the x~ changing facts, on the ground and in the clouds.

Our neutral state of being disregards
past and future.

Illusions, no more

"Creativity is intelligence having fun."

———

Surely, creative fun is the nectar of life.

Through the power of change and exchange we can begin to understand Darwin's Evolution.

At the time, it was an absurd notion not to obtain a free ticket to Darwin's hall of fame for his succinct Natural Selection, by plying the oceans of evolution; watching Waves turn Particles, seconds turn minutes in the deep eons of Darwin's fertile imagination!! Good deed indeed. It must have been fun.

As for my fun, I sometimes enjoy imagining, my surreal self being a hummingbird, when in reality I evolved to be a Bower bird...

In my natural nesting ground,

of course.

"The idle man does not know what it is to enjoy rest."

———

Ideally, an idle life can also be a source of joy. A concept I famously imbued in my deliberate way of thinking ~ feelings ~ being.

So far my idleness often triggers my advanced creative imagination. Everything is nothing and nothing is everything. The zero is my creative ascent to the everything 010 totality.

Energy I.S. Matter mischievously turned 10 dimensional, a code deciphering our inseparable reality from illusions. From nothing to something.

The Tangible 1 juggles the Intangible 01 ~ Timing

"A hundred Times every day I remind myself that my inner and outer life are based on the labors of other men, living and dead, and that I must exert myself in order to give in the same measure as I have received and am still receiving."

———

Not unlike you Albert, I also stand tall on the shoulders of giants like you, I get so much for nothing, other than living by the grace of my intangible essence, soul, spirit and mind.

Values are not what an individual can give or take. The best value is our integral part of the total humanistic values. The kind you have thrown at us over your right shoulder.

Thank U

"I believe in intuitions and inspirations. I some-times feel that I am right. I do not know that I am."

———

Intuitions and inspirations are the holy grail of our inseparable mental and G.U.T. functionality.
We are pixels run by cosmic Ouroboros.

The 01 feed on one another, a combined Life ~ Force behind the T.E.N. Dimensional Universe.

'The Eternal Now' is home to our Now Reality Shaw.

We drink water loaded with intuitions, we breathe ions remembering digital memories; a case which leads us to wander through the many worlds of wonders. Huffing and puffing digital ions into thin air, and into the known.

Breath well, be inspired

The Neutral Zone

"When I am judging a theory, I ask myself wheth-er, if I were God, I would have arranged the world in such a way."

———

Hi again Doctor,

God is not in the arrangement business. God is the arrangement. And you doctor have been an integral part of this amazing scientific arrange-ments, your algorithmic formulations informing us to form, reform, and **inform**.

Your kind of Digital Fermentation was your own judgment on your theorized arrangements, imbued by the holographic vibrations of your brilliant, albeit, virtu-al violin.

It must have been fun to requiem your
physical escape.

extremely nice

"A question that sometimes drives me hazy—am I or are the others crazy?"

Foggy, when I am hazy I feel as if I am crazy.
When I feel crazy my thoughts and feelings go numb, foggy and hazy.
Hazy and crazy seem to be swinging hither and tither as unattached fuzzy spider web acting my hustling and bustling neurons.
I am a subject to my incoming thoughts, which are not mine. How do they Quantize my ephemeral temporal feelings? And how in the world do thoughts and feelings discreetly seep into my being, the biodegradable machine that I am?

My thoughts appear and disappear between my ieys and ears while the neural lines traverse between moving pictures frames, riding my mental waves.

Wow~ But how does it do it?
Even my council Chris Jones and his cat Audrey have no idea.

Rest assured Albert, all the others are the crazy 1nes,
except for the cat

"The only thing more dangerous than arrogance is ignorance."

—

If we combine arrogance and ignorance we will then notice a conflict between our mental neurons and the ions of our breath.

When I don't understand totality I feel as if I am in Heisenberg's State of Uncertainty, being and not being. Like a cat in a guessing box that poses the deepest question about life, minus death.

Can an innocent cat decipher its unknown fate?

It's a spooky case of being virtual in streaming vernal thoughts.

Better yet,
Wisdom and joy are flowering spirit and mind.

Trust in Time
expect the unexpected

"No problem can be solved from the same level of consciousness that created it."

——

Sir,
As a doctor you have given us a dose of split human consciousness to a point of relativistic schizophrenia.

Let's remember that in modern Times, neural consciousness is not a human problem, human illusions certainly are.
Furthermore, God is a dangerous word, Timing is not. Timing is our realistic illusions. No one can see God in motion because God IS the motion.

God is a brightly acting star, and we are the blind sub actors, trying to chase chicks in holy woods.

We experience synchronization of the unknown. Erroneously beg for God's help, but ultimately we alone must grapple with the mysterious God, remembering the God of the Bible who said, don't eat from the tree of knowledge…

So, I tick tock the tree of wisdom

"Information is not knowledge."

———

The Incoming thought formations reform the forms, informing us about the wider, brighter, and the formation of knowledge.

Understanding the Kabbalah of Information, is the first and the last link in understanding the chain of Creation. Our understanding of totality augments the unity of our fractured beliefs and human knowledge.

Understanding is hermetic and complete, up to the 01 Planck point of life's synergy.

Wisdom is self-imaging ~ cosmic-memories. Information can be reconceived, or, continue to live in our animalistic fertile imagination.

I revel in my conscious feelings with my whimsical Being ness

knowledge I.S. Information

Information I.S. knowledge

"To punish me for my contempt for authority, fate made me an authority myself."

———

Fate is my highest authority.

I am well fated to be naked and neutral.
No sins, no fig leaves and no impending punishment.
When I have no say in the matter, I just follow the cues of whatever emerge as a Being.
I ask myself; Who is the one in driving seat, if not my digital ieye?

As soon as fate shackles the pixels of my authority, I cut the chain and flee, if I can. Or just surrender by redeeming my-own authority; paying a non-denominational ransom.

Otherwise, I resort to paying my ransom in

Biblical Shekels

"Science without religion is lame, religion without science is blind."

———

The cane cannot walk without the lame, the blind cannot see with glasses.

Religion dampens realities -- culminating in a climatic clash of civilizations; judged by the criminal courts of the immoral and the unjust.

But who is to Judge the judges??
(The ICC Suddenly comes to mind!)

There is a need to amalgamate science and philosophy in order to understand the evolutionary ~ creativity of our collective minds.

The Quanta is now opening the gates to our broader fields of vision into a new quantized consciousness

Religiosity is but a Voodoo peering into our Belief Systems

"If the facts don't fit the theory, change the facts."

——

In order to balance our consciousness, we can either conjugate the facts with the theory, or change the theory to fit the x change.

The Tower of Babble came tumbling down because some elves did not understand the effect of cohesive mumbling. There was no one to translate 0s and 1s, without GPS

(God's P.S. = Gravitational Propulsion System)

As such, any mumbling can lead to a meltdown of frozen mentality, whether it occurs in Ur, Babylon, or in Jerusalem.

Icy facts on the ground

"If you can't explain it simply, you don't understand it well enough."

———

Creation is the human mind acting in accordance with Quantum Mechanics. Impacting our evolutionary trend of Thought; From hunters ~ gatherer to Neanderthals to the biological robots that we are today. Switching to Timeism to experience the newer paradigm where us being the robotic aliens we are searching for.

We are as all other aliens, we are Biological Beings fostering a new industrialized robotics humanlike paradigm. We all live in quantized 01 Timing Zone, switching between tangible and Intangible. Timing Time in Action.

I found that the simpler the Truth is, the harder to get to the bottom of it. Especially when there is no bottom to G.U.T. feelings at the end of Pi.

However, if you try to explain the 01, and/or the I.S. to a 3 years old child he/she will 2 understand.

Movements are creative beauty
Choreograph your child to be a genus not a terrorist

"Relativity applies to physics, not ethics."

———

From early age, teach the young to comprehend the simplicity of 01 Relativity. So they too, can acquire an understanding needed to lead to a life of creative fulfilment.

General relativity implies everything IS Relative, including physics, philosophy, morality and ethics. Ni ~ Ai and Pi = iP.
Infinite Possibilities are the Grand Relativity of our collective minds.

Pure intellect needs a geek to understand the potential, as everything is bunched up as:
$$Ni \sim Ai \,\&\, Pi = iP$$

As above so below, so is our American
Pi in the sky

In Time, Judaism is the natural expression of God's ~ Creation. We all live in quantized Timing Zone ~~ switching between Time and Timing, and suddenly, we find ourselves embedded in a memory stick. We are all the images of our forever Souls, spirits, and mind of the Universe.

"A new type of thinking is essential if mankind is to survive and move toward higher levels."

Our **Binary** Thought comes in two flavors, bits and bytes, pixels and pixelates, a neutral split between negative and positive.
The negative creates the positive up to oblivion and back again, as if nothing has happened.
No discount
The hot and the cold, the yes and no, thinking and feeling, Time and Timing, all are dignified in one single Quanta ~ called singularity.

Life is T.E.N. Dimensional Bytes infiltrating national boundaries, as 2wo cosmic minus crossing to *Be the +*.

From simplicity to complexity, the androgynous God twirls into double helix, Being of man and woman, inadvertently.

The intersexing of two intangible cosmic minuses breed the tangible + plus.

~~+ +~~

"The whole of science is nothing more than a re-
finement of everyday thinking."

―――

The whole of science is to polish human comprehension, to refine some not so glorified BS Ideas.

Our minds trick us by sequestering reality in a holographic entanglement created by our infinite Ka-
leidoscopic vision. Dark energy in Black hole
searching for our unstable selves and twitching
Thought, harboring other thoughts, all in
tim0second singularity.

Life is the soul of virtual memories
crowned by spirited virus galore

I have no choice but to cling to everything I remember, or say.

"I assert that the cosmic religious experience is the strongest and the noblest driving force behind scientific research."

———

Yes,
Your cosmic religious experience was your driving force up to your Nobel Prize entitlement for physical Entropy. ~~~

Congratulations!!

Novel Entropy
Yin & Yang

Intangible

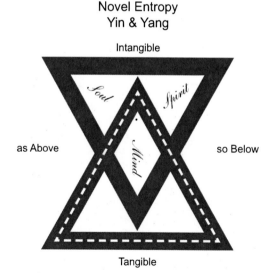

as Above   so Below

Tangible

"The grand aim of all science is to cover the greatest number of empirical facts by logical deduction from the smallest number of hypotheses or axioms."

———

Divide 0 by 0 and get an ultimate deduction.

Baby Bangs are the final axiom to clear the debris of our deeply ingrained beliefs in a Big Bang.

Besides, Albert, you have left us with mc^2 as your final axiom but now there are few other axioms that can be reduced down to the G.U.T. of Matter and Energy, Space and Timing.

The T.O.E. IS helping science to uncover the hidden 01 in the G.U.T. of singular holes, veiling the Truth about Gravitational Synergy.

We encompass tiny black holes of neurons in our brains, creating and destroying at once. Leaving us with 01 Quantum potential to grapple with.

~ Creation ~~ Evolution ~~~ Entropy

From 0 we come to 0 we go

"I lived in that solitude which is painful in youth, but delicious in maturity."

———

Of course,
You enjoyed your solitude because you allowed yourself to think deeply about Thought, without BS and any of its demagogical interpretations.

As for me, other than fully enjoying my life experiments, I also enjoy my solitude by digging deeper into my exuberant feelings absent of thoughts.

Emancipation at last

U can not be but Be
I cannot be but Be,
Free

"If you want to live a happy life, tie it to a goal, not to people or things."

———

Simply, life IS pain and joy.

Throughout life I lacked any diploma. So I went experimenting with what comes my way. And yes, I moved from failure to success to failure, and to success again, all while having no goal in mind.

My life followed some whimsical taste for ethical beauty, which at Times have failed me. But luckily I succeeded in maintaining my posture, balancing between the am and the I.

No question asked.

Happiness is a temporary sense of joy. It opens and closes the gates of my pain and joy without any attempt on my part to mess with my precious Neutrality. Neutrality IS King.

And here is the acute beauty of my joy, I find joy and beauty not in my cup of coffee, but in my
G.U.T.

Grand Unified Theory ~ Electro Magnetism

"Never give up on what you really want to do. The person with big dreams is more powerful than one with all the facts."

———

Dreams fall short of doing. I discovered that my doing is instrumental to my ongoing state of Being.

Things, big and small show their growth, but not how they grow!

Accordingly,
I resort to minimizing my doing, realizing that *everything happens by itself,*
I live my life, I grow and die by myself, driven by the the neutral Life Force

Proof: Look around and witness how everything is moving in accordance to the Timing of non-minute power.

The power of ephemeral reverse causality

If I desire to discover that which may come next;
I consult with my autonomous G.U.T. Feeling
Premonitions are the inception of Thought,

~ My Creative Potential ~

"Although I am a typical loner in daily life, my consciousness of belonging to the invisible community of those who strive for truth, beauty, and justice has preserved me from feeling isolated."

———

I have nowhere to go or hide other than in the sanctuary caves of my on/0f defusing mind.

In the crevasses of my mental caves I feel least isolated ~ even in the dark except for a tiny shimmering romantic light.

~ my memories ~

It cannot be any deeper than deep

"I do not at all believe in human freedom in the philosophical sense. Everybody acts not only under external compulsion but also in accordance with inner necessity."

———

My inner necessity for "Free Will" is no other than free choice. The will is totally free and subject to a personal choosing. Yes, or no. The "will" does not author my willing, it is but the desire to choose the willing.

Will or no will. We are all prisoners of our synaptic neural psychosis. In a philosophical sense there is no free will other than free choice, naturally switching on and Of between approval and disapproval, assisted by reflections of Pain and joy.

Either or neither…   ha …

Feelings are the deterministic author of our driven desires, choice and action. I am slave, subject to the Timing of my inner neutral switching conundrum. Timing I.S. the functionality of my Being. which makes me what I am. We are the reflection of our thoughts ~ translated to Be: 'We are that we are'.

"Free will" is a fantasy

"Let us not forget that human knowledge and skills alone cannot lead humanity to a happy and dignified life."

———

Knowledge and skill is what make humans happier, especially when we understand it in binary terms.

Our dualistic world heightens our awareness to what already I.S. ~~ digitized world of fidgeted Information.

010 paves the new ways for us to decipher our digitized telepathic communication

```
    0
  0 1 0
    0
```

G.U.T. ~matter ~ energy.

"He who can no longer pause to wonder and stand rapt in awe, is as good as dead; his eyes are closed."

———

The Universe is the quintessential thinking machine playing dice.

God I.S. rapt in awe when he closes his eyes, while euphorically playing his humble violin.

And suddenly playful vibration gone silent

"It is, in fact, nothing short of a miracle that the modern methods of instruction have not yet entirely strangled the holy curiosity of inquiry."

In fact, the large hadron collider has been doing just that. Strangling the holy discovery of the Quanta ~ the foundation of the already Quantized world of re ~formation.

The greatest discoveries have been smothered by scientists trying to nullify, or ignore the Quanta for being the God of all mathematical axioms.

Whether consciously or subconsciously, the LHC kept running for the sake of keeping the economy going.

All in All, it makes sense

Science must hunker down for survival

"The only real valuable thing is intuition."

———

Premonition is subconscious intuition tunneling out to the manifestation of Thought.

We emit and receive information while we are being informed by neutral formations, formulating the on/0f switching events.

Nothing can be static. Everything changes. Even Nothing flickers between light and dark.

The 1 something and the 0 nothing do constantly create and vigorously evolve. Not unlike struggling salmon swimming up waterfalls to reach their spawning riches, only to perish and die in total fulfillment.

Life is suspended between
Positive and Negative
Light and Dark,
Life and Death
Yes, and No

~

Free your mind, expect the unexpected!

"Make everything as simple as possible, but not simpler."

———

Humans are the simplest links that connect the first and the last link in the chain of Creation.
When my mind grinds out a new idea, I distill this idea still further, polishing and re-polishing until it shines to its highest degree of Truth; So you the reader can easily comprehend the essential ingredients streaming through the waves of your own mind.
A being bound to get lost between the invisible memories of yore and perceived future. Not unlike the separating lines between moving pictures in a movie streaming through your mind...
Ephemeral moving lines are where the changing pictures between the lines makes you think that those moving pictures are real, which make you feel entertained.

Footnote:
You may want to watch 'the Astonishing Simplicity of Everything' on youtube.com: Presented by the eminent physicist Neil Turok. An excellent presentation where you'll find the simple Truth that will compel you to step down from your high pedestal to a level of being simple.

"Invention is not the product of logical Thought, even though the final product is tied to a logical structure."

———

The logical emanates from the illogical.
The 1 emanate from 0. A sacred path running through the back door of our consciousness rather than through the already open gates to a fresh air where flowering sanity thrives afield.

My logical structure flickers along the shimmering neurons of my crown jewel ~ Amygdala,

Originally, Creation was introduced by father Abraham the Jew

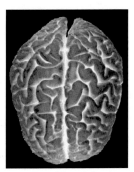

Gray Singularity

"Any intelligent fool can make things bigger, more complex, and more violent. It takes a touch of genius, and a lot of courage, to move in the opposite direction."

———

Like me, even a fool can sometime encounter some simple stroke of genius.

A genius is one who is courageous enough to avoid conflicts and inner emotional confrontations.

Peace

Inner conflicts no more

01 Deep Mind

"Look deep into nature, and then you will understand everything better."

———

I don't jeopardize my endowment as a *neutral* being, because I cannot ignore being ~ natural.

I look deeply into nature it helps me shine the limelight on the neutral nature of my emerging minute - Life.

Neutral mind mines Time

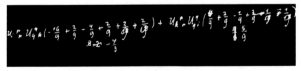

Einstein's deathbed equation.

"Imagination is everything. It is the preview of life's coming attractions."

———

Creation is the inception of bewitched *ions* reforming our coming attractions.

Premonitions are the inception of imagination leading us to creative bright Ideas.

The thoughts of our warbling imagination constitute the ultimate attractions the kind we seek throughout life.

Thought formations are the gateway to pure consciousness.

A ghostly reaction to The Eternal Now

Reality

"God does not play dice with the Universe."

———

Super women have super minds, they play the chess of life.
Men just throw the dice.

If humans play dice which they do, it follows then that…

God plays dice too

~

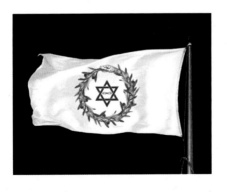

"Strive not to be a success, but rather to be of value."

———

I strive to be of reason before I understand its value, knowing that every reason knocks out a million other concealed reasons.

The Quanta IS the Initial Creation process

Entropy IS when the + plus and the -- minus go oblivion,

01 dualities back to 0

An acknowledgment of ephemeral Being

"Once we accept our limits, we go beyond them."

___

When I reach the top of my limit, I jump over the precipice into a void of no limit.

This allows me to observe my Timing at work ~ to change according to the exchanging rate of my polarized being:

A Mind simulation for not knowing
that which they already understand

Imagination is more important than knowledge. Knowledge is limited. Imagination encircles the world."

———

Sure, imagination can roam the world while knowledge is segmental and conditional.

"I believe in this and that, I know this and that, but I don't comprehend the eminent nature of Totality"

Imagination can get stuck being compartmentalized in a singularity that punches *holes* in our bubbling - thinking neurons.

Knowledge may constrict our imagination, but our imagination can envision the unknown and:

un ~ expected *Premonitions*

"A clever person solves a problem. A wise person avoids it."

———

Yes, but I still have the urge to decipher the enigma of how the flower grow!

That is to say, beyond the consumption of water, soil, air, and sun.

How do they do it and what mechanism drive their G.U.T. and their life force?

I have no idea.

In order to understand the expanding nature of the big bang, we first must understand the origin of the amazingly riche ness of life, the infinite self creation 01 Baby Bangs.

Creation I.S. constant

Evolution is intermittent

"The great moral teachers of humanity were, in a way, artistic geniuses in the art of living."

——

The best living art is to *Be* the living Gods that we are.

Life is art, God is art, and you Albert were the greatest moral artist of them all.

Thank you doctor

No death, no life

"I have no special talent. I am only passionately curious."

———

Your curiosity took you to the endless bottom of knowledge before you discovered the final stretch to the bottom less passion of the unknown,

Curiosity and passion ~ united

Soul and Spirit vibrate the neurons
of your creative Mind

The Wrestling Within, a painting by the author

"A man should look for what is, and not for what he thinks should be."

———

Indeed, I view all things as they are.
(our planet is but a seed, a seminal to future habitable planets... Maybe)
I am who I am in accordance with the Biblical treatment of my creative soul. For millennia we have been trying to decipher Kabbalah. Now Eduard Shyfrin has opened the floodgates to Kabbalistic Creation, the I.S. -- Information System, reforming the course of Mental Therapy.

In his book *'From Eternity to Man'* Eduard Shyfrin places the Information System at Quantum level.
Forming and reforming, Creation to generation, Waves turn Particles.
The I.S. is our wakeup call, alerting the hallucination of our mental deformity.

Beliefs were the Manna which helped humans discover Quantum Mechanics, altering our way of thinking, or walking the deserts of the unknown.

The Thought x~Change is the I.P. that was and

always will Be

"The ideals which have always shone before me and filled me with joy are goodness, beauty and truth."

———

Goodness and beauty are two sides of the same coin. Their circumference is the Gorilla glue joining heads and tails, beginning and end.
No infinite circumference, no duality ~ no coin.

Even so, with all the coins in the world, my creative genius is quite unbelievable.

People call me the Absurd Edmond Cohen.
I love it.
The Absurd will be the title of my next book.

Doctor, regardless; People like me were climbing your philosophical sturdy step ladder of which each step ascends me to a higher - magical joy and goodness, the hermetic silent Truth.

Thank you

Harmony is an undeniable Truth.

I~Dia – U~Dia

"If you are out to describe the truth, leave elegance to the tailor."

——

Of course,

First, I must tailor the tailor, or find a tailor who's familiar with the inner Universal algorithmic compositions.

When I seek elegant truth, I first must find whether the truth can be *redressed*, or whether the truth is comprehensible.

Timing tames the tailors

"Great spirits have always encountered violent opposition from mediocre minds."

———

It is not unlike the eruption of violent volcanos where mediocre / fascist minds leave the world without headstones, and great minds resort to scatter their ashes?

When vessels shatter ~~ few urns may still be intact but buried under the sand.

"I believe in standardizing automobiles. I do not believe in standardizing human beings."

———

Genetically speaking,

Our neutral Natural ~ Intelligence (NI) is the double helix that standardizes us all ~ differently.

   You and I doctor have no say in the matter.

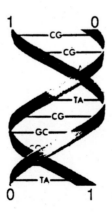

"Concern for man and his fate must always form the chief interest of all technical endeavors. Never forget this in the midst of your diagrams and equations."

———

The conscious ~ subconscious human interest is fate.
Both are based on diagrams, equations, and blazing algorithmically shifting spirits.

Fibonacci Sequence in a nautilus shell

"Weakness of attitude becomes weakness of character."

———

And yet,

Acknowledging our weakness strengthens our character and resolve. Leading us to a newly inspired emancipation to pass-on to future generations.

Watch out for danger

One rotten demagogue can spoil generations of Established Truth

"The difference between stupidity and genius is that genius has its limits."

———

Stupidity also has its limits.

Stupidity and genius both are subject to human erroneous mental combustion.

No creative wisdom is deeper than the deepest wisdom of the **collective** human mind.

We are IT

Stop Slow Down
A painting by the author

"The only source of knowledge is experience."

—

Experience is a tool that we must remember how to optimally use. Otherwise, knowledge is a waste of Time, waste of energy, memory loss, and a lack of momentum.

Not my momentum

*"The important thing is to not stop questioning.
Curiosity has its own reason for existing."*

———

Curiosity is the bread and butter of our intellect
which needs to be digested before gestation.

A good reason for our motivational coexistence is
our natural ~ neutral sense of gravitational cooperation.

Positive human cooperation is the measure
of humanity's success.

"Each of us has to do his little bit toward trans-forming this spirit of the Times."

———

On my part, the least I can do is share my blazing ideas in written words explaining the Timing factor of the T.E.N. Dimensional Universe ~ 'The Eternal Now' future ~ past duality.

There is no present per se. All is ephemeral.

Whether alive or dead movements are the x change of natural coexistence in the Quantized nature of Timing.

Each movement is a moment of Creation

"Science can flourish only in an atmosphere of free speech."

ACHTUNG !!
Science is precise, free speech can be imprecise and dangerously hazardous to our mental health and social order.

Remember!!
The Germans formed the "Arbeit Macht Frei," which is a horrendous form of forced labor. The killer of humanity's highest aspirations ~ freedom.

History attests that most free speeches harness pedagogy and shiploads of political BS diplomacy which tend to smother our lives, furthering away our joyous endeavors.

Throughout history, Democracies have been abused by charismatic demagogues (...Hitler) who took humanity to the brink of oblivion, committing genocide to near total annihilation.

Beliefs are not facts

They are transient and conditional,

hindering human development!

"Unthinking respect for authority is the greatest enemy of truth."

———

Authorizing any and all Belief Systems should be un-authorized and declared as such, and to be incarcerated out of the way.

All *unrealistic* Beliefs should be declared un-Kosher and abolished as mediocre policies.

BTW...
here is the grand gender gap

*If you **trust** in Creation you are a Jew*
If you believe in Evolution you are a Jewess
while Creation evolve.

"Few are those who see with their own eyes and feel with their own hearts."

———

Perception and feelings are the substrates of our existence ~ a bittersweet subconscious excitement.

My fun experience, is when my heart is beating and can breathe normally without 0, and still be able to walk naked and yell

aha...

Eureka ~

I breathe digital i~ons

"It's not that I'm so smart, it's just that I stay with problems longer."

———

Doctor,
You were smart to distill and redistill your source of truth by discovering that the unknown is the ultimate Truth.
Even God of the Jewish Bible have said "Don't eat from the Tree of knowledge".

The unknown is the gateway to understanding the inflated secrets as to how God's Mind Works.

Knowledge is but a segment of axiomatic theories, which eventually lead us to understand the wisdom of what I.S. a Being and what not a being.

On that note:

God's absurdity should not be the U.N.S.C. Standard Bearer.

"The only thing that interferes with my learning is my education."

———

We come into life to say hello, make waves, learn and teach others how to swim in turbulent white waters. Then, with a smile we reach the river delta saying hello and goodbye to oceanic memories.

I remember
Waters remember.

Doctor, I speculate that it must have been your great joy to discount your education post receiving your post doctorate, stamped... Nobel Prize.

Thank you Nobel
You were dynamite

"Most people say that it is the intellect which makes a great scientist. They are wrong: it is character."

———

Intellect and character are united specialties.

Although, sometimes they turn out to be the Achilles heel that digs into our confidence, and hinder our understanding of Totality.

Moreover,
No great, or even mediocre scientist can separate his character from his intellect.

Characteristically, no intellect can survive the onslaught of murderous fascists and barbaric book-burning characters.

Terrorism is not Allah's moral imperative.

Peace

Shalom

Salam

"A happy man is too satisfied with the present to dwell too much on the future."

———

A happy man has no need to dwell on future, knowing that everything is switching in the eternal now reality.

Past and future are ephemeral virtual realities that appear and disappear, at once without notice.

On the other hand

When a man is squeezed between the eternal now and then, he too will be satisfied to know that there's no present, realizing that the ephemeral now has just passed on ~ unto the unknown.

I was privileged to discover the true nature of Time
when my grandfather clock chimed
midnight, Venice Mean Time
Sep. 18 ~ 19 ~ 1979

Not Greenwich Mean Time

"Learn from yesterday, live for today, hope for to-morrow."

———

I took a furlough from the shackles of my hopes, which destined to drag me behind.

So 'y' hop?

Hope is a wishful thinking, short of brewing my hops.

Things, do happen by them selves, they are self ~ created, self ~ designated.

With the Crown Virus in the air, I refuse to shop for hop when there is no sobering fact that it can lead me to where I rhythmically would like to be,

Reasoned and seasoned

Mathematics reforms the forms

forming thoughts into Ideas

"Don't listen to the person who has the answers; listen to the person who has the questions."

———

As all the animals in the world, we also have stereophonic ears…
… let's hear them both

Do insects have ears?

Do pixels have eyes?

"All that is valuable in human society depends upon the opportunity for development accorded the individual."

———

The development of an individual, cross ~ pollinates our social structure, revealing some unexpected geniuses like you, a one who did the creative work and moved us along to the new paradigm.

Learning from history allows us to stand on the shoulders of giants like you, Albert.

Geniuses are few in the world

"One flower is beautiful; a surfeit of flowers is vulgar."

———

Surfeit flowers are the rainbow of the earth... whether one, two, or a million.

Flowers are givers.

Instinctively, Sofia, my niece's 3 years old daughter loves to pluck them as she walks the Venice canals of Venice, for their sensuous scent, delightful colors and fascinating shapes.

But we are still facing the conundrum of how flowers grow!!

Flowers shrivel to dreams and then...
poof - fades away

"You never fail until you stop trying."

—

As a primordial Jew I never try. I just am, doing what I *must*. As God said, stuff your i in the am so you can Be... truly yours.

The Creation concept has been ingrained by primordial Judaism following Father Abraham's footsteps, way before Darwin's Theory of Evolution. The Jews adopted the am and termed it יהוה ~ **Time as Yahweh,** Thus if you **Trust in Time** you are a Jew.

In Time, the Jews accepted Creation as an undisputable Truth. Their religious belief is evident in their traditions, passion and zeal.

Consciously and subconsciously, Jews and non Jews have no choice but **Trust** in Time.

The Torah has led science to flourish with metaphors, equations and axioms. The most notable are posted as mc^2 followed by ∞^2 and by the entanglement of Space ~Time duality

We are all Time Element

Soul ~ Spirit ~ Mind ~ United

"Long live impudence! It's my guardian angel in this world."

———

Dear Albert,

MC^2 was your impudence, my ∞^2 is my guardian angel.

MC^2 and ∞^2 are now humanity's redeeming axio-matic angels.

$$Time = MC^2 = Infinity\ Squared$$

"I am by heritage a Jew, by citizenship a Swiss, and by makeup a human being, and only a human being, without any special attachment to any state or national entity whatsoever."

———

Bravo doctor,

History attests to the fact that Father Abraham revelation of Creation happened even before the Mesopotamians discovered the 0, and thousand years before the Hindus.

Christianity and Islam emerged latter based on Jewish attributes ~ Creation and Evolution.

There is no doubt, the concept of Free and Democratic world IS a Jewish concept.

The discovery of the 01 closes the digital cycle of life and death, Creation ~ Evolution = Entropy.

No more pretentious mischievous U.N.S.C.

The UN un-Democratic Demagogy should not be a playing field of death.

"I love to travel, but I hate to arrive."

—

Doctor,
Have you ever been in touch with your premonitions?

In your next life, when you have a G.U.T. Feeling of impending disaster advise your captain to change course to avoid hitting another tip of another **titanic iceberg**.
Or… stay put where you come from.

Travelers beware

always expect the unexpected

Life can be dangerous

"Life is like riding a bicycle. To keep your balance, you must keep moving."

___

Enough riding for now. For the last few centuries we have been going extremely fast. Let's slow-down.

Now I have to stop and take a break, remembering that movement and rest are subject to the relativistic centrifugal cosmic forces.

Therefore I might change my bicycle for a scooter with a fully depleted batteries!

How fun...

"I'm doing just fine, considering that I have trium-phantly survived Nazism and two wives."

——

As to "Nazism Final Solution";
De~brain the Nazis of their screwed pixels and pixelates.

Your free mind Albert, was the measure of your success, by fleeing the claws of Nazis and their <u>insane</u> methods of atrocity and genocide.

Of course, Nazi Beasts with their unrestrained Ideology have disturbed your joy and creative life, but your two wives gave you moments of respite and peace.

Now you are safe and secure

Rest in peace

No complaints

Nothing lasts forever ~ only nothing lasts

"I have finished my task."

———

I salute you, Doctor!
It was a phenomenal miracle how you thought about Thought's functionality. Your creative genius is still valued as templates for our scientific and philosophical development.

You were trying to fill the neutral gap between the 0 and the 1 in the attempt to dig up the 010 theoretical black holes of eternity.

Here is an idea… In your next Life, when you want to fully understand how Big Bangs work, stuff one of them tightly with a newly born Baby Bangs (photons) it will give you a better chance to celebrate the bonanza of your relativistic finale`.

Alive or walking dead, we are living history.
So now I am writing my eulogy in un ~
nuanced theme

Until then,
Ai ~ Ni Sir

APPENDIX

And now,
At the end of Time ~ Timing has taken over to establish coherence between humanity and the singular dominant Godly ~ Universe.

Electro ~ magnetism
Quantized ~~ Thought
Quantized ~~ Mind
Quantized ~~ Time

God's mind IS represented by the gravitational collective mind of humanity.
Timing R ~ us
Small and big black Holes united turned White Holes of Quantized Gravity

As all the animals in the world,
so we are in the Timing Zone
And here is a dead question to answer past innumerable deaths.

Who won and who lost the barbaric wars?

Do you care?

From the news

The Jerusalem Post
January 30, 20/21

by Zachary Keyser and Yonah Jeremy Bob

Quantum is the state of things being unknown at the subatomic level until they can be observed and move from the byte to the "qubit." In a Quantum computer, it is said that the values assigned to 0 and 1 can occur at the same Time. The reason the impossibility is possible is because of the Quantum's subatomic level where protons and electrons are acting in a wild way beyond the rules of nature as we tend to think of them. Picture the Avengers' superhero Antman shrinking into the Quantum zone where Time does not even move in a linear fashion.

Quantized Timing!

The Cosmic Switch

The cosmic Switch IS the Timing of the at-once
Infinite Potentials. We are the creative Mind of
Quantized ~ universe.

Everything, and every moment falls
within the realms of the Infinite Possibilities

The University of Time offers to mend a desperate
world.
Let's enhance the wellbeing of our creative juices,
by *slowing the* path of destruction.

**Thoughts are Information Memory
as Neutral as the Universe
Scientific Truth down to the Quanta**
~
Belief systems are just that... B.S.

Live the images of your mind
your thoughts ~ the God within
your visions
Everything is predicated on Timing,
and you are I.T.

The Time GENESIS

The Neutral Life Force

Digital memories

~ Quantum Split ~
in our memory bank
regurgitated memories
quantum energy
singularity
thought
a bit
of In~Formation

Everything I.S.
Reformed infinite possibilities
ephemeral switching Bi ~ on and 0f

Don't rush, there is no Time, everything runs by Timing,
synchronized energy ~ matter ~ to be,
I am who I will be ~ you will be as you will Be
your eyes are the eyes 0f God

Animals are in touch with their inner world
Humans are in touch with their outer word.

Writing is my Sovereignty

∞^2

G.U.T. ~ Q.M.

MC^2 ~ G.R.

Evolution

Genesis

Theory of Everything

TIMIMG

Tree of Life

Time is irrelevant

Experience The Living Truth

Time is Illusion ~~ Timing is reality!

Glossary

0: Time, Space, Nothing; Intangible, Absolute Vacuum.

1: Tangible, Energy, Matter, Universe.

01: The complementary binary, the unifying force.

Baby Bang: A Quanta or Singularity where the inception of photons takes place.

B.S.: Belief System; Beliefs and Superstitions.

Creation-in-Action: The moment-to-moment Creation process.

Freedom of Mind: Not thinking you are the thinker.

G.M.: Good Morning, Grand Master.

G.U.T.: Grand Unified Theory.

I.B.M.: "I" Bio-Machine.

I-Dea: Implies I-Goddess (masculine: I-Dio)

Infinity Squared (∞^2): Infinite Time multiplied by Infinite Possibilities.

In-Formation: The formation of energy.

Instinct: The culmination of total information in the fraction of a second.

I.P.: I Photon; Infinite Possibilities; Infinite Potential.

I.S.: Information System; Infinity Squared.

I.T.: Information Theory.

The M Theory: Magic ~ (highlighted in pink).

The Mind: The combination of soul and spirit.

Neutrality: The absolute balance between universal polarities.

Quanta ⁓: A unit of Thought. A leap from 0 to 1. Cosmic potential.

Quantum Mechanics (QM): The Dualistic Universe acting within the constraints of the Intangible-Tangible duality; Infinite Potential.

Thought: The interaction between bits of information to Be (what I.S.).

Time^2: Timing.

Timeism: A comprehensive understanding of Creation.

Timing: The algorithmic rhythm of computing change and exchange.

T=mc^2: Time equals Mass times the Speed of Light Squared; Thought equals Mind Capacity Squared.

T.O.E.: Theory Of Everything.

Totality: 01 (the in-tangible tangible Uni-Verse).

Universal Computer: The total Timing Machine.

Books by Edmond Cohen

Man I.S. the Last to Be Tamed (1983)
Time: The Total Mind (1988)
The Universe I.S. Made of 0s & 1s (2014)
7 Booklets of Aphorisms (2015)
01 Uni-Verse (2016)
The Hole Book: 3 Books in 1 (2017)
Edmond Cohen: Art (2018)
Conversations with a Physicist: Book 1 (2019)
Conversations with a Physicist: Book 2 (2019)
Conversations with a Yogi (2019)
Conversations with a Poet (2020)
Conversations with a Rabbi (2020)
Conversations with a Lawyer (2020)
From the Alleys of Baghdad (2020)
My Rapport with the Spirit of Albert Einstein (2021)

Videos by Edmond Cohen

Neutral Paradigm (Universe) (2015)
Our Minds in Time (2014)
The Dali Hama on the Binary Universe (2015)

www.universityoftime.com

Read and watch free of charge!

OR, ORDER ON AMAZON!

Made in the USA
Columbia, SC
06 October 2022